FROM ZERO TO ONE AND BEYOND

FRACTIONS, DECIMALS, AND PERCENTS

MathScape
SEEING AND THINKING MATHEMATICALLY

PHASE**ONE**
Fractions from Zero to One

In this phase you will develop your fraction sense so that you are able to recognize and write equivalent fractions, compare fractions, and think about "hard" fractions by using easier fractions that they are close to. You will use what you learn by using fractions to represent data you collect on a topic of your own choice.

FROM ZERO TO ONE AND BEYOND

How are fractions, decimals, and percents related?

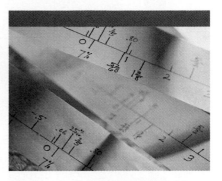

PHASE**TWO**
Percents from Zero to One

Percents are another way of representing parts of a whole. You will explore equivalent percents for familiar fractions. By the end of the phase, you will have collected 60 to 90 pieces of data on a topic you have chosen. You will use what you learn to represent the data as percents and display it on a "fraction circle" graph.

PHASE**THREE**
Decimals from Zero to One

In Phase Three, you will develop strategies for renaming a fraction, decimal, or percent in either of the other two ways. You will transform fractions to decimals or percents, percents to fractions or decimals, and decimals to fractions or percents. The secret is in understanding how fractions, decimals, and percents are related.

PHASE**FOUR**
Beyond Zero and One

What lies beyond zero and one on the number line? You will see what happens when the number line is extended beyond 0 and 1 in both directions. Then you will zoom in closer and closer on the number line. Some interesting questions will come up as you look deeper and deeper at the numbers between numbers.

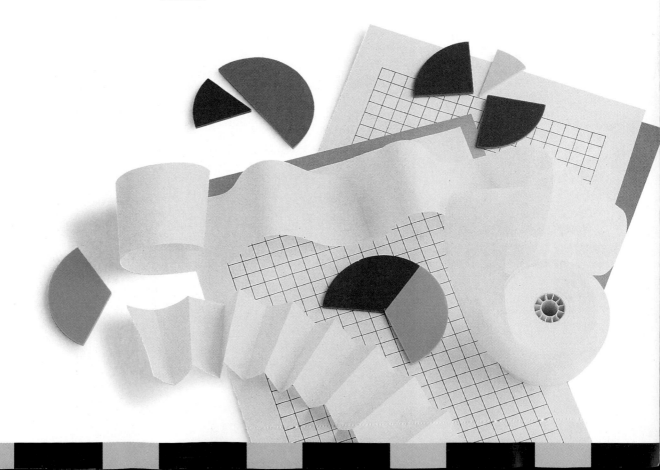

PHASE ONE

Fractions are one way to represent the relationship between a part and a whole. In this phase, you will use fractions to label distances between 0 and 1 on a number line. You also will use fractions to label parts of a circle and describe a set of data.

When you cook from a recipe, write a check, fill a gas tank, or describe the results of a survey, understanding fractions can help you make sense of the world around you.

Fractions from Zero to One

WHAT'S THE MATH?

Investigations in this section focus on:

NUMBER and NUMBER RELATIONSHIPS

- Recognizing and writing equivalent fractions
- Comparing and ordering fractions
- Finding patterns in equivalent fractions

DATA

- Using fractions to describe data
- Sketching fractional parts of a circle to represent data

 # Folding Fractions

FINDING PATTERNS
IN EQUIVALENT
FRACTIONS

You will make a Collections Report about real-world data over the next several weeks. You will describe your data in different ways, starting with fractions. Your exploration of fractions begins with making a fraction strip and looking at fractions that name the same number.

Make a Fraction Strip

What fractions can you show by folding a strip of paper?

A fraction strip is a useful way to show fractions. Follow the steps below to make your own fraction strip using a long strip of paper.

1 Mark 0 on the left corner and 1 on the right corner of the strip as shown.

2 Now, fold your strip *exactly* in half. Unfold the strip and write $\frac{1}{2}$ on the fold.

3 Fold the strip again to show a different fraction. Then unfold the strip and write the fraction that fold represents.

4 Continue folding and labeling your strip to show as many fractions as you can. Be sure to fold carefully—when you fold your strip into fourths, all four parts of your strip should be the same length. Also, don't forget to label each new fraction you make.

Organize Lists of Equivalent Fractions

Look at one of the folds on the fraction strip you made. All of the fractions you wrote along the fold are equivalent fractions. Make a list of the equivalent fractions for several folds on your strip.

How are fractions that represent the same number related to each other?

1 Find the fold on your fraction strip that shows the most fractions. List all of the fractions on this fold in order. Be sure to start with the fraction that has the smallest denominator and end with the fraction that has the greatest denominator.

2 Look for a pattern in the equivalent fractions you listed. Do any fractions seem to be missing? Insert these fractions in the list.

3 Now, extend your list by writing the next two fractions in the pattern.

4 Repeat Steps 1–3 to make lists of equivalent fractions for at least four of the folds on your strip.

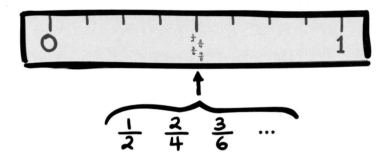

How did you use patterns in equivalent fractions to help fill in and extend your lists?

Write About Equivalent Fractions

Now that you've explored equivalent fractions, write about what you've learned.

- Choose a fraction that is *not* on your fraction strip. List at least four fractions that are equivalent to this fraction. Then explain how you found the equivalent fractions.

- Describe how you could find an equivalent fraction for any fraction you are given.

hot **words** | fractions
equivalent fractions

Homework

page 36

 # Fraction Circles

If you have $\frac{5}{8}$ of a stick of butter, can you make a recipe that calls for $\frac{3}{4}$ of a stick of butter? It's important to be able to decide if two fractions are the same size or if one is greater. In this lesson, you'll use Fraction Circles to explore fraction equivalence and inequality.

Find the Greater Fraction

How do you know which of two fractions is greater?

Fraction Circles or sketches can help you decide which of two fractions is greater.

Use Fraction Circles or sketches to solve and create "Which is greater?" questions.

1 Think about each question. Then write a statement using $<$ or $>$ to answer each one.

a. Which is greater: $\frac{3}{4}$ or $\frac{1}{4}$? **b.** Which is greater: $\frac{5}{9}$ or $\frac{2}{9}$?

c. Which is greater: $\frac{2}{5}$ or $\frac{3}{5}$? **d.** Which is greater: $\frac{3}{8}$ or $\frac{1}{4}$?

e. Which is greater: $\frac{1}{2}$ or $\frac{1}{3}$? **f.** Which is greater: $\frac{5}{8}$ or $\frac{5}{6}$?

g. Which is greater: $\frac{3}{5}$ or $\frac{3}{4}$? **h.** Which is greater: $\frac{7}{10}$ or $\frac{14}{22}$?

2 Now, write three "Which is greater?" questions of your own. Trade questions with your partner, and answer each other's questions by writing a statement with $<$ or $>$. When you are done, explain how you knew which fraction was greater.

Inequalities

Inequality signs are used to show how numbers compare. The smaller part of the sign points toward the lesser number.

- We read $5 < 8$ as "Five is less than eight."

- We read $3 > 1$ as "Three is greater than one."

Make and Solve Fraction Puzzles

In this investigation, you will make and solve fraction puzzles about equivalence and inequalities.

How can you find fractions that are equal to, greater than, or less than other fractions?

1 Create three fractions puzzles about equivalent fractions.

  a. Sketch a fraction on a piece of paper. Write the name of the fraction under the sketch.

  b. Write an equivalence statement for the fraction, but leave either the denominator *or* the numerator blank. (Be sure you can solve the puzzle!)

  c. Exchange puzzles with your partner. Fill in the blank to solve your partner's puzzle. Use Fraction Circles or sketches to show why your answer is correct.

$$\frac{1}{2} = \frac{}{4}$$

2 Write three puzzles using a < or > sign. Exchange puzzles with your partner and solve your partner's puzzles. Use Fraction Circles or a sketch to show that your answer is correct.

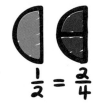

$$\frac{1}{2} = \frac{2}{4}$$

3 Now, write a fraction puzzle that you think will stump the class. Again, be sure that *you* know the answer to your puzzle.

$$\frac{1}{3} < \frac{}{4}$$

Write About Fraction Equivalence and Inequality

Write about what you have learned about fraction equivalence and inequality.

- Write a list of "dos" and "don'ts" for finding equivalent fractions. Be sure to include sketches to illustrate your ideas.

- Tell how you can decide which of two fractions is greater if they have the same denominator and different numerators. What if two fractions have the same numerator and different denominators? Don't forget to explain your thinking.

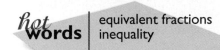

hot **words** | equivalent fractions
inequality

Homework

page 37

3 The First Collections Report

REPRESENTING DATA AS FRACTIONS

Some fractions, such as $\frac{1}{2}$ and $\frac{1}{3}$, are so familiar that most people find it easy to think about them and compare them. Other fractions, such as $\frac{11}{23}$ and $\frac{8}{19}$, are not so familiar. It is easier to think about an unfamiliar fraction if you can identify a familiar fraction that is equivalent or close to it.

Make Fractions More Familiar

How can you make a less familiar fraction easier to think about?

Use what you know about equivalent fractions to find more familiar ways to name unfamiliar fractions.

1 With a partner, find familiar equivalent fractions for at least *four* different fractions.

- Choose a number from the "numerators" list below. Have your partner choose one from the "denominators" list. Then use these numbers to write a fraction.

  Numerators: 3, 6, 9   Denominators: 18, 24, 36

- Rewrite this fraction with the smallest denominator that you can. Make sure that this more familiar fraction is equivalent to the original fraction.

2 For a fraction that does not have a more familiar equivalent, it can be helpful to find a more familiar fraction that is close to it, or approximate. Find approximate fractions for at least *four* different fractions.

- Choose a number from the "numerators" list below. Have your partner choose one from the "denominators" list. Write a fraction using these numbers.

  Numerators: 5, 7, 11 Denominators: 23, 32, 43

- Find a more familiar fraction that is close to this fraction. Then write a sentence explaining how you found this fraction.

Compare Familiar and Unfamiliar Fractions

In each fraction pair listed below, one fraction is familiar and the other is unfamiliar. Pick one pair and decide which of the two fractions is greater. Then explain the strategy used.

a. $\frac{1}{2}, \frac{11}{23}$
b. $\frac{1}{8}, \frac{8}{27}$
c. $\frac{1}{6}, \frac{2}{11}$

When two fractions are very close, how can you tell which is greater?

Make a Collections Report

It's time to write a report about the data you have collected so far. Follow these steps to help you put your report together.

1 Write a summary of your data that answers these questions.

- How did you collect your data?

- How many pieces of data have you collected so far?

- How many categories do you have? What are they?

- How many pieces of data are in each category?

2 Use fractions to describe your data.

- Use a fraction to describe the part of your data in each category.

- For each fraction you used to describe your data, name a more familiar fraction that is *equivalent* (with a smaller denominator) or that is *close to* (approximates) the fraction.

3 Sketch circle pieces to illustrate your results.

- Sketch a fractional part of a circle to represent the data in each of your categories.

- Label each of your sketches with the category and the fraction it represents.

hot **words** | numerator
denominator

Homework

page 38

PHASE TWO

1996 U.S. imports from sub-Saharan Africa

Nigeria 38%

Angola 18%

Others 16%

South Africa 15%

Gabon 13%

Total: $15.2 billion

Source: Commerce Department

Percents are another way to represent the relationship between a part and whole. How are percents related to fractions? You will find out as you rename percents as familiar fractions they are close to.

You can see percents all around you—representing data in newspapers, in magazines, on television, even on your favorite cereal box. You will use percents to represent the 60 to 90 pieces of data you collect on a topic of your choice.

Percents from Zero to One

WHAT'S THE MATH?

Investigations in this section focus on:

NUMBER and NUMBER RELATIONSHIPS

- Understanding the meaning of percent
- Finding or estimating the percent of space taken up by a shape
- Comparing and ordering percents
- Finding an exact or approximate percent name for a fraction

DATA

- Using percents to describe data
- Creating circle graphs to represent data

4 Out of One Hundred

EXPLORING PERCENTS BETWEEN ZERO AND ONE

A percent describes a portion of a whole quantity that has been divided into 100 equal parts. By investigating the percent of space taken up by a shaded region, you will get a better idea of how the sizes of different percents compare.

Create Percent Designs

What do different percents look like?

You will be given handouts of large and small 10-by-10 grids. Use the blank grids to make designs that meet the following descriptions.

1 Use the small grids to create a design for each description below.

    a. 20% shaded

    b. 33% green, 67% yellow

    c. 15% red, 30% blue, and 55% yellow

    d. 25% red, 40% blue, 30% green, 15% yellow

2 Choose your favorite design from the grids you colored in Step 1.

    a. Copy your favorite design onto the large grid handout.

    b. Compare the large and small copies of the same design. Look at the areas that are shaded the same color. How are they alike? How are they different?

Estimate Percents Visually

You found the percent of space covered by different figures on a grid. Now you will estimate percents for shapes of your own that aren't on a grid.

How well can you estimate percents without a grid?

1 Each member of your group should draw a "blob" on the Estimate Percents Visually sheet, and shade it in.

2 As a group, estimate the percent of the paper that each blob takes up. Write this percent on the line "First Estimate."

3 Now put your blobs in order from smallest to largest percent. What do you notice about the percents that go with the blobs?

4 With your group, use a grid transparency to revise the percent estimate for each of your blobs. Do this by placing the grid over your blob and finding the percent of space the blob actually takes up. Write your new estimate on the line "Revised Estimate." Look for patterns in the differences between your first estimates and your revised estimates. For instance, were your original estimates always too high or too low?

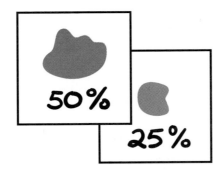

Write About Percents

Imagine this: What if the same size and shape blob you made appeared on a much larger piece of paper?

- Would the percent covered by the blob on the larger paper be equal to, greater than, or less than the percent that you estimated it covered on the smaller paper? Explain your answer.

- Can 50% of something ever be less than 25% of something else? Explain your answer.

hot**words** | percent

Homework
page 39

5 Percents That Make Sense

RELATING PERCENTS
TO FRACTIONS

You used Fraction Circles to explore equivalent fractions for familiar fractions. Here you'll use Fraction Circles to name equivalent percents for familiar fractions. Your knowledge of these percents will help you estimate percents for other fractions.

Label Fraction Circles as Percents

How can you show percents as part of a circle?

For this investigation, you will use Fraction Circles pieces to help you think about percents.

1 Organize your Fraction Circles. Decide what percent each piece represents. (For some pieces, you may want to choose a percent that is close to the right number.)

2 Make sketches of all the Fraction Circles pieces. Label them with their percent names. Be prepared to explain how you decided what percent name to give each color of Fraction Circles piece.

3 Sketch some circle pieces that are not in the set. Label them with their exact or approximate percent names.

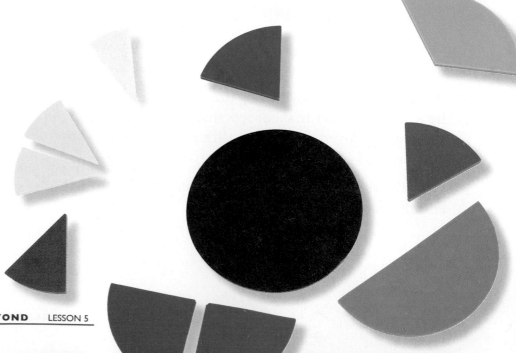

Estimate Percent Equivalents for Fractions

It's helpful to be able to make a rough estimate of the percent name for a fraction. For instance, knowing that pizza represents $\frac{101}{120}$ of all food-to-go orders may be harder to think about than knowing that about 85% of such orders are for pizza.

Look at the fractions you and your classmates came up with. Work with a partner to do the following:

1 Choose three or four of the fractions.

2 Estimate the percent name for each of the fractions you chose. (Hint: You already know percent names for several familiar fractions. Can these help you begin to make your estimates?)

3 Discuss how you would explain your estimation method to other students. You may be asked to do this when you report your estimates to the class.

How can you estimate the percent name for an unfamiliar fraction?

Write About Fraction/Percent Equivalence

In your own words, answer the following questions.

- What strategies did you use to find percent names for Fraction Circles pieces?

- Is there a quick way to tell whether or not a fraction is easy to name with an exact percent? If so, describe how.

- How can you estimate the percent name for an unfamiliar fraction?

hot**words** | percent

Homework

page 40

6 The Final Collections Report

REPRESENTING
DATA AS PERCENTS

Many people find it easiest to think about data when it's described as percents. In newspapers and magazines, graphs of data make reports especially easy to understand. Here, you will use percents to report your Collections Report data and to help make circle graphs.

Represent Data on a Circle Graph

How can you use a circle graph to show data?

For her Collections Report, one student gathered data on the different things that her classmates collect. The table below shows her data.

Topic: Student Collections

Category	Number	Approximate Percent
Sports Cards	12	13%
Coins/Stamps	57	61%
Comic Books	12	13%
Stuffed Animals	8	8%
Other	5	5%

1 Find a Fraction Circles piece or combination of pieces that is close to each percent in the table.

2 Try to assemble a circle using these fraction pieces. If you have gaps or overlaps, can you tell where these come from?

3 Using your Fraction Circles pieces as a guide, sketch a circle graph for the data.

4 Color your graph. Then label each part of the circle with the percent it shows and the name of the category it represents.

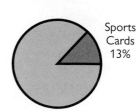

Sports
Cards
13%

Use Percents to Make a Collections Report

How can you use percents to help describe your data?

In your first Collections Report, you described your data using fractions. Now you will make a Collections Report using percents. In this report, you will use what you know about percents and their fraction equivalents to describe the data.

Be sure to include the following in your report.

1 Write a summary of your data that answers these questions:

- How did you collect your data?

- How many pieces of data have you collected?

- How many categories do you have? What are they?

- How many pieces of data are in each category?

2 Use percents to describe your data.

- Use a fraction to describe the part of your data in each category.

- Then, give an exact or approximate equivalent percent for each fraction.

3 Make a circle graph to show your data.

- Choose Fraction Circles pieces to make a circle graph of your data. Some pieces may be exact, some will be approximate.

- Make a sketch to show your circle graph. Label the sketch with both fractions and percents.

hot **words** | percent
circle graph

H•mework

 page 41

PHASE THREE

You have seen how to use fractions and percents to name the same number. In this phase you will use a third way to represent part-whole relationships: decimals.

There is no way that is always the "best way" to represent a number. But sometimes one way of representing a number is better in a certain situation. Can you think of different situations in which you would choose to use fractions, decimals, or percents?

Decimals from Zero to One

WHAT'S THE MATH?

Investigations in this phase focus on:

NUMBER and NUMBER RELATIONSHIPS

- Understanding decimal representations of numbers between 0 and 1

- Developing strategies for renaming decimals as percents and percents as decimals

- Using division to rename fractions as decimals

- Understanding how to write a repeating decimal

- Using place value to rename terminating decimals as fractions

- Ordering a mixed set of fractions, decimals, and percents

7 An Important Point

Fractions and percents are two ways to represent numbers between 0 and 1. When you write a part of a dollar, you use a third way to represent a number—a decimal.

Make Fraction/Decimal/Percent Puzzle Pieces

How can you name part of a 10-by-10 grid as a fraction, decimal, or percent?

For this investigation, you will use 10-by-10 grids to explore fractional, percent, and decimal representations for the same number.

1 Cut out the four grids. Take two of them, and leave the other two for your partner.

2 Cut one of your grids into four "puzzle pieces." Cut along the lines, so your pieces are made up of whole squares.

3 On each puzzle piece:

- Write the fraction of the original square that it represents.

- Using the fact that the original square represents 100%, write the percent name for the piece.

- Write the decimal name for the piece.

4 Repeat Steps 2 and 3 for your second grid. Make different-size puzzle pieces than you did the first time.

5 Mix up the eight pieces from your two puzzles. Exchange puzzle pieces with your partner, and assemble each other's puzzles. As you do this, check to be sure that you agree with the fraction, decimal, and percent names on each piece.

Investigate Decimal Equivalence

Earlier in this unit, as you explored fractions, you found patterns that helped you write lists of equivalent fractions. Here you will look at equivalent decimals.

How are decimals that represent the same number related to each other?

1 Cut and label pieces from 10-by-10 grids to show each of the following amounts if the 10-by-10 grid is one.

   a. 0.04   **b.** 0.40   **c.** 0.4   **d.** 0.040

2 Compare the pieces of grid paper you cut and labeled.

- Were any of the decimal amounts equivalent?

- For any equivalents you find, write two more decimals that would also be equivalent. Explain your thinking.

Place Value in Base 10

To be able to give the decimal name for a fraction like $\frac{3}{10}$, $\frac{77}{100}$, or $\frac{833}{1,000}$, you need to know how place value works in decimal numbers.

When we say the number 9,471 aloud, we hear place values: "Nine thousand four hundred and seventy-one." Each step to the right divides the place value by 10.

Place value also tells us how to read digits to the right of the decimal point. The 5 in the number 0.542 represents five tenths, the 4 represents four hundredths, and the 2 represents two thousandths. Again, each step to the right divides the place value by 10.

$$\underline{9,471.}$$
thousands hundreds tens ones

decimal point (not always shown)

We use the last digit when we say a decimal number aloud. This number is, "five hundred

$$0.\underline{542}$$
ones   tenths hundredths

decimal point   thousandths

hot **words** | decimal system   equivalent

Homework

page 42

Tenths, Hundredths, and More

You know the percent and decimal names for some familiar fractions. You also know how to estimate percent names for unfamiliar fractions. In this lesson you will use more exact ways to rename fractions, decimals, and percents.

Rename Some Twelfths and Twentieths

How many percent and decimal names for twelfths and twentieths can you find?

You will be given the handout Twelfths and Twentieths. Use everything you know about equivalent fractions and percent names for familiar fractions to fill in as much of the table as you can.

1 Look at the fractions in the Twelfths and Twentieths table. Do any of these have more familiar equivalent fractions?

  a. List all of the more familiar equivalents you can find in the box with that fraction.

  b. Fill in as many percent names as you can for the fractions in the columns labeled "Percent Names." Circle any percents you write that are approximate.

2 Use what you know about place value to fill in decimal names for fractions on your Twelfths and Twentieths table.

  a. Some of the fractions in your table can be renamed as tenths. Fill in the decimal names for all of these fractions. Be sure to write a 0 to the left of the decimal point.

  b. Now, fill in decimal names for as many of the other fractions in the table as you can.

Fraction Names	Percent Names	Decimal Names	Fraction Names	Percent Names
			$\frac{11}{20}$	
$\frac{1}{20}$			$\frac{7}{12}$	
$\frac{1}{12}$			$\frac{12}{20}$	
$\frac{2}{20}$			$\frac{13}{20}$	
$\frac{3}{20}$			$\frac{8}{12}$	

Complete the Twelfths and Twentieths Table

You can think of a fraction as a division problem. For example, $\frac{3}{4}$ is another way to write $3 \div 4$. Thinking of fractions in this way can help you complete your Twelfths and Twentieths table.

1 Fill in any missing numbers in the "Decimal Names" columns of your table by using a calculator to divide the numerator of the fraction by its denominator.

2 Find places where you have already written both the decimal and percent names for a fraction. Check to see that these numbers make sense.

3 Now fill in any missing entries in your "Percent Names" columns.

How can you use division to rename a fraction as a decimal?

Write About the Renaming Process

So far, you have used a variety of methods to rename fractions, decimals, and percents. Use what you have learned to write about the different methods.

- Write a set of renaming rules for the methods you've investigated.

- Which methods do you think you would choose to use most often? Does it depend on the situation? Tell why.

Repeating Decimals

Some decimal names for fractions have a repeating pattern that goes on forever. For instance,

$\frac{1}{3} = 0.33333333333333333333333333333333$ ... (forever!)

When this happens, you can write the exact decimal name by using a bar to show the repeating digits. Be careful to put the bar only over the digits that repeat.

- $\frac{5}{12} = 0.416666... = 0.41\overline{6}$

- $\frac{3}{11} = 0.272727... = 0.\overline{27}$

hot **words** | repeating decimal equivalent

H omework
page 43

All Three at Once

You know how to rename fractions as decimals, decimals as percents, and percents as decimals. Now, you will explore ways to rename a decimal as a fraction. Finally, you will use your renaming skills to put a mixed list of fractions, decimals, and percents in order.

Find Fraction Names for Decimals

How can you use familiar fractions to rename decimals?

In this investigation, you will rename decimals as exact fractions and familiar fractions that are easier to think about. Start by making a table with three columns as shown.

1 For each decimal, find an *exact* fraction name, and enter the name in the table.

Decimal Name	Exact Fraction	Familiar Fraction
0.26		
0.71		
0.14		
0.44		
0.08		
0.65		
0.31		
0.86		
0.548		
0.367		

2 Now, find a familiar equivalent fraction (smallest denominator) or a more familiar fraction that is close to each decimal. Add these fractions to the table.

How do you know that your fractions are the *closest*?

Order Fractions, Decimals, and Percents

Here you use what you know about fractions, decimals, and percents to put a mixed group of numbers in order.

1 Cut out the numbers on the handout Ordering Fractions, Decimals, and Percents. Use any strategies that you find helpful to put these numbers in order from least to greatest. As you work, think about ways to convince your classmates that your order is correct.

2 Once you are satisfied with your list, make a written copy of your final ordering.

How can you put a list of fractions, decimals, and percents in order?

hot **words** | equivalent

Homework
page 44

PHASE **FOUR**

Now that you have investigated numbers between zero and one, it's time to go beyond. When you extend the number line in both directions, you will learn about other ways of representing numbers.

Why are there so many ways to show the same number? It's because we need to use numbers in so many different ways. As you learn new ways to show numbers, think about the advantages and disadvantages of all the different ways to represent numbers.

Beyond Zero and One

WHAT'S THE MATH?

Investigations in this phase focus on:

NUMBER and NUMBER RELATIONSHIPS

- Renaming improper fractions as mixed numbers and mixed numbers as improper fractions

- Comparing negative numbers

- Finding exact or approximate square roots

- Calculating powers

- Locating a mix of numbers on a number line, including fractions, decimals, percents, improper fractions, mixed numbers, negative numbers, square roots, and powers

10 Going Beyond

EXPLORING
NUMBERS GREATER
THAN ONE AND
LESS THAN ZERO

So far in this unit, you've investigated numbers between 0 and 1. Here, you will look at fractions that describe numbers greater than 1. After investigating numbers greater than 1, you will explore negative numbers—numbers that are less than 0.

Investigate Mixed Numbers and Improper Fractions

How can you rename a mixed number as an improper fraction or an improper fraction as a mixed number?

In this investigation, you will look for relationships between mixed numbers and improper fractions.

1 For each number below:

- if it is a mixed number, rename it as an improper fraction.
- if it is an improper fraction, rename it as a mixed number.

(Hint: It may help to use Fraction Circles to represent some of these numbers.)

$$\frac{5}{3} \quad 1\frac{1}{6} \quad \frac{7}{4} \quad 2\frac{3}{8} \quad \frac{37}{10}$$

$$5\frac{1}{2} \quad \frac{38}{5} \quad 4\frac{5}{6} \quad \frac{26}{4} \quad 3\frac{1}{5}$$

2 Use your adding machine tape to make a number line. Mark 0 in the middle of the line. Then add marks for the whole numbers 1 through 10.

3 Now locate each of the numbers in Step 1 on your number line. Write both an improper fraction and a mixed number name for each.

Mixed Numbers and Improper Fractions

There are two different ways to write fractions greater than 1.

- A number that contains both a whole number and a fraction, like $3\frac{1}{3}$, is a mixed number.

- A fraction whose numerator is greater than its denominator, like $\frac{7}{4}$, is an improper fraction.

Play the "Which Is Greater?" Game

All negative numbers are less than 0, but some are "more less" than others! In this investigation, you will think about inequalities involving negative numbers.

How can you write inequalities involving negative numbers?

1 Add the numbers −5 and −10 to your number line.

2 Write a statement using < or > to answer each question. You may want to refer to your class number line as you think about these.

  a. Which is greater: −3 or 9?

  b. Which is greater: 0.01 or −7?

  c. Which is greater: −2 or −8?

  d. Which is greater: −9 or 3?

  e. Which is greater: −6 or −1?

  f. Which is greater: $-2\frac{1}{2}$ or −3?

  g. Which is greater: −8.74 or −8.05?

3 Mark the numbers in these inequalities on your number line.

4 Now, write three "Which is greater?" questions of your own. Trade questions with your partner, and answer each other's questions by writing a statement with < or >.

5 With your partner, discuss any rules for ordering negative numbers that you think you have discovered. Be prepared to share your ideas with the class.

Negative Numbers

A number that is less than 0 is a negative number. Every negative number can be thought of as the opposite of a positive number. For example, the opposite of 3 is −3.

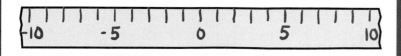

hot **words** | improper fractions
mixed numbers

Homework
page 45

11 Root for Yourself

When you find the square of a number, you ask, "When I multiply this number by itself, what do I get?" When you look for the *square root* of a number, you ask, "What two numbers, multiplied together, give me my original number?" You will investigate square roots and how to find them.

Investigate Square Roots for Perfect Squares

What is a perfect square?

Complete the tables on the handout Square Roots. Follow these steps to explore why the numbers in the right-hand column of your completed table are called perfect squares.

1 Think of each small square on your 10-by-10 grids handout as a "unit square." Choose a perfect square number from your table. Can you cut a square out of one of your grids that contains this number of unit squares? If you can, cut out the square.

2 Make as many different-size squares as you can with your four grids. (Cut along the lines—no half-squares allowed!)

3 The area of a square is equal to the number of unit squares it contains. Find the area of each of your squares. How does the area of the square compare to its side length?

Squares and Square Roots

Squaring a number means multiplying the number by itself. For example, 5^2 is 5×5, or 25. The square root of 25 is 5. The $\sqrt{}$ sign is called a *square root* (or *radical*) sign. $\sqrt{25}$ asks, "What number, multiplied by itself, equals 25?"

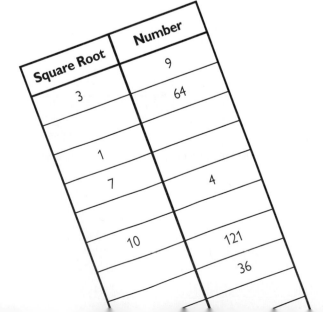

Square Root	Number
	9
3	64
1	
7	4
10	121
	36

"Zoom In" on Square Roots

The numbers below are not perfect squares.

How can you find the square root of a number that is not a perfect square?

1 Use the "zoom-in" method to locate the square root of each of these numbers. Sketching number lines will help you. For each number, stop when you have "zoomed in" to the hundredths place.

a. 27   **b.** 48   **c.** 83

d. 111   **e.** 54.68   **f.** 10

2 Write a short description of how you located each of the square roots.

Write About Square Roots

Suppose you are given a number that is not a perfect square. In your own words, explain how you would find its square root to the nearest hundredth.

Zooming In

For numbers that are perfect squares, you can use the "zoom-in" method to locate the square root.

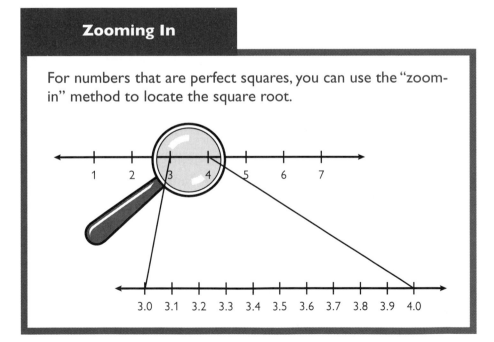

hot **words** | perfect square
square root

page 46

12 Powering Up

You know that a power describes how many times a number is multiplied by itself. Here, you will investigate how quickly repeated multiplication makes numbers grow. After exploring powers, you will place a mix of different types of numbers on one number line.

Locate Powers on the Number Line

Are powers of a number evenly spaced on a number line?

In this investigation, you will use a strip of adding machine tape to show the part of a number line that goes from 0 to 1,000.

1 Measure or fold your tape so that you can locate the numbers 100, 200, 300, ..., 900 accurately. This is your "power line"!

2 Without calculating any powers, guess the highest power of 2 that fits on this segment of the number line. For instance, is 2^{100} the last power of 2 that is less than 1,000? Or is the real answer more like 2^{30} or 2^{500}?

3 Starting with 2^1, find all of the powers of 2 that fit between 0 and 1,000. When you have found them all, mark them on the number line in the same color. (Hint: Remember that $2^1 = 2$.) How close was your guess from Step 2?

4 Repeat Step 3 for the other whole numbers from 3 to 10. Use different colors to mark the different power families on your power line.

How do powers grow as the exponents increase?

Place Different Numbers on a Number Line

In this unit, you have worked with fractions, decimals, percents, mixed numbers, improper fractions, negative numbers, square roots, and powers. Now you will demonstrate some of what you have learned by placing numbers of each of these types on a number line.

1 Make a number line that shows the numbers from −10 to 10.

2 Place each of the following numbers on this line. Be sure to show the original form of the number, even if you renamed it in another way to help you see where it belonged.

−8	$\frac{3}{7}$	0.75	50%	−1
$1\frac{1}{5}$	$\frac{7}{3}$	$\sqrt{64}$	2^2	$-5\frac{3}{4}$
$\frac{35}{48}$	0.09	9%	−3	$7\frac{3}{8}$
$\frac{57}{10}$	$\sqrt{22}$	3^2	−0.8	2^3

How can you use your knowledge and strategies to place several different types of numbers on a number line?

hot words | exponent powers

omework

page 47

Folding Fractions

Applying Skills

1. Name three equivalent fractions for each fold on the fraction strip shown.

$$0 \quad \frac{1}{8} \quad \frac{1}{3} \quad \frac{1}{2} \quad \frac{3}{4} \quad \frac{14}{16} \quad 1$$

For each fraction listed, give four equivalent fractions. Then place each list in order. Be sure to start with the fraction that has the smallest denominator and end with the fraction that has the greatest denominator.

2. $\frac{2}{3}$ **3.** $\frac{1}{9}$

4. $\frac{3}{8}$ **5.** $\frac{1}{4}$

6. $\frac{7}{8}$ **7.** $\frac{2}{4}$

8. $\frac{4}{11}$ **9.** $\frac{5}{10}$

Provide the next two fractions in each list of equivalent fractions.

10. $\frac{1}{4}, \frac{2}{8}, \frac{3}{12}$ **11.** $\frac{1}{3}, \frac{2}{6}, \frac{3}{9}$

12. $\frac{1}{2}, \frac{2}{4}$ **13.** $\frac{2}{7}, \frac{4}{14}$

14. $\frac{2}{3}, \frac{4}{6}, \frac{6}{9}$ **15.** $\frac{4}{5}, \frac{8}{10}, \frac{12}{15}$

16. $\frac{1}{10}, \frac{2}{20}$ **17.** $\frac{5}{7}, \frac{10}{14}$

Extending Concepts

All of the fractions listed are equivalent to each other except for one. Find the one fraction that does not belong in the list.

18. $\frac{1}{5}, \frac{2}{10}, \frac{4}{12}, \frac{5}{25}, \frac{3}{15}$ **19.** $\frac{1}{8}, \frac{3}{24}, \frac{2}{16}, \frac{5}{30}, \frac{4}{32}$

20. $\frac{2}{3}, \frac{6}{9}, \frac{4}{6}, \frac{8}{10}, \frac{10}{15}$

21. On the fraction strip shown, the fractions in red are correct but several of the fractions listed as equivalent are not. Find each fraction that is not equivalent to the fraction listed in red above it.

0	$\frac{1}{8}$	$\frac{1}{3}$	$\frac{1}{2}$	$\frac{3}{4}$	$\frac{14}{18}$	1
	$\frac{1}{16}$	$\frac{2}{6}$	$\frac{3}{6}$	$\frac{4}{8}$	$\frac{7}{8}$	
	$\frac{2}{16}$	$\frac{3}{8}$	$\frac{4}{8}$	$\frac{6}{7}$	$\frac{8}{9}$	

Writing

22. Name three examples where it would be useful to know equivalent fractions.

23. Answer the letter to Dr. Math.

> Dear Dr. Math,
> My brother said that $\frac{1}{2}$ is equal to $\frac{4}{8}$. I don't see how that could be, since 4 is bigger than 1 and 8 is bigger than 2! Who's right?
> Sincerely,
> Fractured Freddie

Fraction Circles

Applying Skills

Use sketches to solve these "Which is greater?" problems. Then write a statement using $<$ or $>$ to answer each one.

1. $\frac{1}{2}$ or $\frac{1}{4}$

2. $\frac{1}{5}$ or $\frac{1}{6}$

3. $\frac{5}{6}$ or $\frac{3}{8}$

4. $\frac{1}{4}$ or $\frac{1}{3}$

5. $\frac{2}{16}$ or $\frac{3}{30}$

6. $\frac{1}{2}$ or $\frac{4}{6}$

7. $\frac{3}{7}$ or $\frac{1}{2}$

8. $\frac{1}{4}$ or $\frac{5}{8}$

9. $\frac{2}{6}$ or $\frac{1}{8}$

10. $\frac{2}{3}$ or $\frac{2}{6}$

11. $\frac{1}{10}$ or $\frac{1}{5}$

12. $\frac{5}{10}$ or $\frac{4}{12}$

Use sketches to help you solve these fraction puzzles.

13. $\frac{1}{2} = \frac{}{4}$

14. $\frac{2}{3} = \frac{}{12}$

15. $\frac{1}{3} = \frac{}{6}$

16. $\frac{3}{8} = \frac{}{16}$

17. $\frac{6}{12} = \frac{}{36}$

18. $\frac{6}{7} = \frac{}{77}$

Solve these fraction inequalities. Use the $<$ or $>$ signs to indicate greater than or less than.

19. $\frac{1}{3} \text{---} \frac{1}{2}$

20. $\frac{1}{8} \text{---} \frac{1}{9}$

21. $\frac{4}{10} \text{---} \frac{2}{3}$

22. $\frac{2}{3} \text{---} \frac{2}{5}$

23. $\frac{7}{16} \text{---} \frac{1}{4}$

24. $\frac{5}{8} \text{---} \frac{1}{7}$

25. $\frac{7}{12} \text{---} \frac{3}{36}$

26. $\frac{6}{7} \text{---} \frac{7}{8}$

Extending Concepts

Solve these fraction puzzles.

27. $\frac{5}{10} = \frac{}{30}$

28. $\frac{7}{9} = \frac{}{45}$

Some of the following statements are true and some are not. Find those that are not true and rewrite them to make them true.

29. $\frac{1}{2} > \frac{2}{4}$

30. $\frac{2}{3} > \frac{4}{6}$

31. $\frac{2}{6} > \frac{8}{12}$

32. $\frac{2}{84} = \frac{1}{2}$

33. $\frac{15}{45} = \frac{3}{15}$

34. $\frac{6}{17} = \frac{12}{34}$

35. $\frac{25}{100} = \frac{1}{3}$

36. $\frac{7}{8} = \frac{9}{10}$

Writing

37. Answer the letter to Dr. Math.

> Dear Dr. Math,
> I have three chores to do on Saturdays: empty the trash, take out the newspapers, and clean my room. My dad says that I'm $\frac{2}{3}$ done after I take out the trash and newspapers. I say that I'm not even half done because cleaning my room takes a lot longer than the other two chores. Who's right?
> Sincerely,
> Tidy Tom

The First Collections Report

Applying Skills

Rewrite each fraction with the smallest denominator that you can. Be sure that each fraction you write is equivalent to the original fraction.

1. $\dfrac{2}{10}$ **2.** $\dfrac{4}{18}$ **3.** $\dfrac{8}{24}$ **4.** $\dfrac{6}{36}$

5. $\dfrac{6}{24}$ **6.** $\dfrac{8}{28}$ **7.** $\dfrac{4}{10}$ **8.** $\dfrac{2}{36}$

Rewrite each fraction with a more familiar equivalent fraction or a more familiar approximate fraction.

9. $\dfrac{2}{4}$ **10.** $\dfrac{6}{11}$

11. $\dfrac{8}{21}$ **12.** $\dfrac{8}{24}$

13. $\dfrac{12}{48}$ **14.** $\dfrac{3}{21}$

15. $\dfrac{4}{16}$ **16.** $\dfrac{9}{80}$

Look at the familiar and unfamiliar fraction pairs. For each pair, decide which fraction is greater.

17. $\dfrac{7}{10}, \dfrac{5}{20}$ **18.** $\dfrac{3}{8}, \dfrac{16}{40}$

19. $\dfrac{27}{81}, \dfrac{3}{91}$ **20.** $\dfrac{14}{63}, \dfrac{36}{44}$

21. $\dfrac{8}{27}, \dfrac{9}{30}$ **22.** $\dfrac{2}{11}, \dfrac{11}{21}$

23. $\dfrac{4}{19}, \dfrac{6}{26}$ **24.** $\dfrac{1}{6}, \dfrac{2}{11}$

Extending Concepts

25. For the fractions listed in items **9–16,** explain how you decided if the fractions could be rewritten with a more familiar fraction that is equivalent (with a smaller denominator) or approximate.

26. For each set of fractions, decide which is the greatest.

a. $\dfrac{2}{10}, \dfrac{2}{11}, \dfrac{3}{12}$ **b.** $\dfrac{7}{21}, \dfrac{7}{22}, \dfrac{8}{25}$

c. $\dfrac{6}{12}, \dfrac{3}{4}, \dfrac{2}{10}$ **d.** $\dfrac{3}{6}, \dfrac{2}{4}, \dfrac{4}{5}$

Making Connections

Dr. Leyva conducted an experiment to see how many orchids would grow in different types of soil. The data he collected is shown in the table.

Soil	Number of Orchids
Moist bark	12
Dry bark	7
Sand	2
Humus	10

27. How many orchids was Dr. Leyva able to grow?

28. Use fractions to tell what portion of the experimental orchids grew in each condition.

Out of One Hundred

Applying Skills

For items 1–4, you will need to refer to the 10-by-10 grid shown.

1. How many squares would you shade in so 50% of the space is shaded?

2. How many squares would you shade in so 20% of the space is shaded?

3. How many squares would you shade in so 10% of the space is orange, 40% of the space is red, 30% of the space is blue, and 5% of the space is purple?

4. How many squares would you shade in so 15% of the space is blue, 30% of the space is red, and 8% is green?

Estimate the percent of space each blob takes up in the squares below.

5.

6.

7.

8.

Extending Concepts

9. What percent of the grid is shaded pink?

10. What percent of the grid is shaded red?

11. What percent of the grid is shaded yellow?

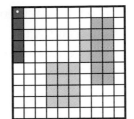

12. What percent of the grid is shaded blue?

13. What percent of the grid is shaded green?

14. What percent of the grid is shaded yellow?

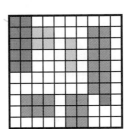

Writing

15. Answer the letter to Dr. Math.

> Dear Dr. Math,
> My mom says that estimating the percent name for a fraction is a useful thing to know. I told her I can't see where or when I'll ever need to know the percent name of a fraction. Could you help me out?
> Sincerely,
> D. Uno

Percents That Make Sense

Applying Skills

For each Fraction Circles piece shown, give the percent each piece represents. If there is not an exact whole percent equivalent, write the percent that is closest.

1.   2.

3.   4.

5.   6.

Make a sketch for each fraction in the list below. Then provide the percent name for each fraction. (For some fractions, you may need to estimate the percent name.)

7. $\frac{1}{5}$ 8. $\frac{4}{30}$

9. $\frac{2}{15}$ 10. $\frac{6}{25}$

11. $\frac{10}{50}$ 12. $\frac{12}{23}$

13. $\frac{3}{20}$ 14. $\frac{44}{49}$

Extending Concepts

Numerators	Denominators
12	20
7	50
13	25
4	80
17	34

15. Use the table to make five fractions.

16. Sketch the fractions and label them with their percent names.

17. What strategies did you use to find the percent names for your sketches?

Making Connections

Mr. Kim owns and operates the food stand for the sporting events at the high school. After the last game, he took inventory to see what sells best. He found that $\frac{9}{10}$ of the hot dogs were sold, while only $\frac{2}{5}$ of the pretzels were sold. He also found that he sold $\frac{4}{5}$ of the lemonade and only $\frac{1}{5}$ of the cola drinks.

18. What percent of the lemonade did he sell?

19. What percent of the cola drinks did he sell?

20. What percent of the pretzels did he sell?

21. What percent of the hot dogs did he sell?

The Final Collections Report

Applying Skills

Maryanne collected data on cat breeds at a cat show. The table shows her data.

Type of Cat	Number
Siamese	20
Calico	12
Himalayan	19
Persian	8
Mixed Breed	39

1. How many cats were at the show?

2. Use fractions to tell what portion of the show was made up of each type of cat.

3. Now give an exact or approximate percent for each fraction.

4. Make a circle graph to show the data.

A team of archaeologists found many items from their last dig. The table shows how they catalogued what they found.

Items Found	Number
furniture	8
clothing	29
cooking utensils	32
other	13

5. How many items did the archaeologists find?

6. Use fractions to describe what portion of the items were of each type.

7. Give an exact or approximate percent for each fraction.

8. Make a circle graph to show the data.

Extending Concepts

A sixth-grade class is baking cookies for a fund raiser. They made a chart to show how many of each type were ordered.

9. Write a fraction to show how many of each type of cookie were ordered.

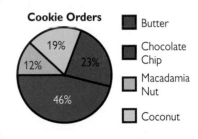

Cookie Orders
- Butter
- Chocolate Chip
- Macadamia Nut
- Coconut

19% 12% 23% 46%

10. If a total of 200 cookies were ordered, how many of each type of cookie will the class have to bake?

11. Because macadamia nuts are expensive, the class would lose money for each macadamia nut cookie they sell. Substituting coconut cookies for orders of macadamia nut cookies, how many coconut cookies will the class need to bake if a total of 100 cookies were ordered?

Writing

12. Answer the letter to Dr. Math.

Dear Dr. Math,
My teacher says that my circle graph should add up to 100%. I say it should only add up to 64 since I only have 64 pieces of information. Who's right?
Sincerely,
Dotty Data

An Important Point

Applying Skills

Use this grid for items 1–6.

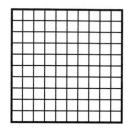

Tell how many squares on the 10-by-10 grid shown you would shade in to represent each decimal amount.

1. 0.08   **2.** 0.80   **3.** 0.8   **4.** 0.080

5. Give the fraction and percent equivalent for each decimal amount in items 1–4.

6. Copy and complete the table by filling in the fraction, decimal, and percent equivalents.

Fraction	Decimal	Percent
$\frac{5}{10}$		
	0.01	
		10%
$\frac{17}{100}$		
	0.62	
	0.030	
$\frac{50}{1,000}$		

$$0.542$$

ones ↑ tenths ↑
decimal point   hundredths ↑
                thousandths ↑

Use the diagram to help you answer the following questions.

7. What is the value of the 7 in 0.375?

8. What is the value of the 4 in 362.4835?

Extending Concepts

9. How many squares would you shade in on the 10-by-10 grid to show each of the following?

a. 0.075   **b.** 23%   **c.** 0.80

d. 0.8   **e.** 0.0750   **f.** 18%

g. $\frac{18}{100}$ **h.** $\frac{23}{100}$

10. Write three fraction and decimal equivalents for 0.070.

11. Explain the strategies you used to find the fraction and decimal equivalents for 0.070.

Writing

12. Answer the letter to Dr. Math.

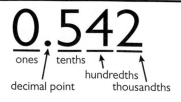

Dear Dr. Math,

My tutor was helping me with decimals. She said that 0.80 and 0.8 have the same value, but 0.08 is different. I told her that couldn't be right. Should I find another tutor?

Sincerely,

Decimal Weary

Tenths, Hundredths, and More

Applying Skills

In items 1–6, give the percent and decimal equivalent for each fraction. Use the bar notation for repeating decimals.

1. $\frac{2}{20}$ **2.** $\frac{3}{12}$ **3.** $\frac{3}{20}$

4. $\frac{4}{12}$ **5.** $\frac{15}{20}$ **6.** $\frac{7}{12}$

Find a decimal equivalent for each fraction below by thinking of each fraction as a division problem. You may use your calculator. Round to the thousandths place if necessary.

7. $\frac{7}{8}$ **8.** $\frac{4}{9}$ **9.** $\frac{13}{20}$

10. $\frac{121}{400}$ **11.** $\frac{18}{33}$ **12.** $\frac{9}{83}$

Use your calculator to check each repeating decimal. If it is not written correctly, make the necessary change.

13. $\frac{1}{3} = 0.03\overline{3}$ **14.** $\frac{3}{11} = 0.272\overline{7}$

15. $\frac{11}{12} = 0.9\overline{16}$ **16.** $\frac{5}{12} = 0.41\overline{6}$

Extending Concepts

17. Find a decimal and percent equivalent for $\frac{200}{323}$. Be sure to round the decimal to the thousandths place.

18. Tell what you did to solve the previous problem. Is your answer exact? Are there any methods that would give a more exact answer?

Making Connections

19. A clothing store is having a sale. The store manager asked one of her employees to make signs indicating the *percent off* for the various items that are on sale. Unfortunately, the employee misunderstood. Correct the signs so they tell the *percent off*.

a. Shorts: $\frac{1}{3}$ off the original price

b. Sweaters: $\frac{1}{2}$ off the original price

c. Shoes: 0.25 off the original price

d. Coats: 0.50 off the original price

e. Shirts: $\frac{2}{6}$ off the original price

f. Pants: $\frac{4}{17}$ off the original price

g. Socks: 0.080 off the original price

h. T-shirts: 0.0770 off the original price

All Three at Once

Applying Skills

Write each decimal as a fraction.

1. 0.6   **2.** 0.06   **3.** 0.98

4. 0.2   **5.** 0.17   **6.** 0.01

Copy the table. For items **7** and **8,** fill in the table as directed.

Decimal Name	Exact Fraction	Familiar Fraction
0.26		
0.44		
0.676		
0.6		
0.903		
0.4		
0.2		
0.334		
0.8		

7. For each decimal listed in the table, enter an exact fraction equivalent in the column "Exact Fraction."

8. Fill in the column "Familiar Fraction" with a familiar equivalent fraction or a more familiar fraction that is close to each decimal. Use the smallest denominator you can. Put a star beside each familiar fraction that is close but not exactly equivalent to the decimal.

9. Write the numbers below in order from smallest to largest.

$$\frac{652}{900}, 0.012, \frac{7}{10}, 32\%, \frac{1}{10}, 0.721, 65\%$$

10. Write the numbers below in order from smallest to largest.

$$63\%, \frac{2}{10}, 0.8, \frac{8}{29}, 85\%, 0.12, \frac{55}{90}, 89\%$$

Extending Concepts

11. How is place value in decimals related to the denominator in an equivalent fraction?

12. Find the decimal name for each fraction listed in the table. You may use your calculator if necessary.

Decimal Name	Exact Fraction	Familiar Fraction
	$\frac{12}{100}$	
	$\frac{2}{10}$	
	$\frac{34}{1,000}$	
	$\frac{2}{8}$	
	$\frac{88}{91}$	
	$\frac{3}{10}$	
	$\frac{4}{5}$	

13. Now, find a familiar equivalent fraction (smallest denominator) or a more familiar fraction that is close to each fraction. Put a star beside each familiar fraction that approximates but does not equal the exact fraction.

Going Beyond

Applying Skills

Rename each mixed number as an improper fraction and each improper fraction as a mixed number.

1. $2\frac{5}{8}$　　　　**2.** $\frac{28}{9}$

3. $\frac{38}{10}$　　　　**4.** $9\frac{2}{9}$

5. $\frac{6}{4}$　　　　**6.** $8\frac{11}{20}$

7. $\frac{44}{8}$　　　　**8.** $4\frac{4}{5}$

9. Sketch a number line from 0 to 10. Locate each of the numbers listed in items **1** through **8**. Write both the improper fraction and mixed number name for each.

10. Tell whether each inequality is true or false. Rewrite the false statements to make them true.

a. $-2 < -1$　　　**b.** $-10 < -5$

c. $-2 > -3$　　　**d.** $-17 > -16$

e. $-2\frac{1}{2} > -4$　　　**f.** $-3.3 < -3$

g. $-1 < -1\frac{3}{4}$　　　**h.** $-6 > 9$

Extending Concepts

11. Place the following numbers in order from smallest to largest.

-1.2　　8　　9.1　　$2\frac{2}{3}$　　-6.7

$-6\frac{4}{5}$　　2.3　　6.7　　-0.021　　$-2\frac{2}{3}$

Making Connections

12. Shabnam recorded the temperature at her cabin in the Sierras for 10 days. The temperatures are shown in the table.

Day	Temperature (Celsius)
1	0.2
2	$2\frac{3}{4}$
3	-1.78
4	$-1\frac{1}{2}$
5	-8.75
6	$-6\frac{3}{5}$
7	-2.6
8	0
9	1.75
10	$4\frac{4}{5}$

Make a number line from -10 to 10 and label the temperatures. For each improper fraction, write the mixed number name. For each mixed number, write the improper fraction.

Root for Yourself

Applying Skills

For each number given, draw a square with sides of the given measure. Then give the area of each square. The first one is done for you.

1. 3 (**Answer:** Area is 9)

2. 5   **3.** 2   **4.** 4

5. 9   **6.** 6

7. Draw a square with an area of 49.

8. Draw a square with an area of 16.

9. Draw a square with an area of 36.

Find each value.

10. $\sqrt{25}$ **11.** $\sqrt{49}$

12. $\sqrt{16}$ **13.** $\sqrt{36}$

14. 5^2 **15.** 10^2

16. 3^2 **17.** 4^2

Extending Concepts

18. What is the relationship between the area of a square and square root?

19. Make a list of the first ten perfect squares. Explain any pattern you see in the numbers.

Making Connections

20. The formula $a^2 + b^2 = c^2$ is used to figure out the length of the sides in right triangles (see the diagram).

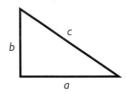

For example, if the length of Side a = 4.47 and the length of Side b is 2.24, you can use the formula to find the length of Side c.

$$a^2 + b^2 = c^2$$
$$4.47^2 + 2.24^2 = c^2$$
$$20 + 5 = c^2$$
$$25 = c^2$$
$$c = \sqrt{25} = 5$$

Use the formula to find the length of the slide shown.

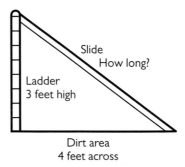

Slide
How long?

Ladder
3 feet high

Dirt area
4 feet across

Powering Up

Applying Skills

Find the following powers.

1. 2^2 **2.** 2^3

3. 2^4 **4.** 3^2

5. 4^3 **6.** 6^3

7. 8^2 **8.** 15^4

Write the expressions for the following:

9. thirteen squared   **10.** eight cubed

11. two cubed   **12.** four squared

In the expressions listed, what is the base? the exponent?

13. 4^3 **14.** 2^3

15. 4^4 **16.** 12^5

17. 3^2 **18.** 6^{10}

19. Make a number line that shows the numbers from -10 to 10. Then place each of the numbers on the line.

$$-6 \qquad \frac{3}{4} \qquad 0.80 \qquad 40\% \qquad -3.5 \qquad 1\frac{2}{3}$$

$$\frac{12}{10} \qquad 2^3 \qquad -2^2 \qquad \sqrt{49} \qquad 78\%$$

Extending Concepts

20. Make a number line that shows the numbers from -100 to 100. Place each of the following numbers in the correct position.

$$\frac{22}{8} \qquad -55 \qquad 0.69 \qquad 35\% \qquad 2^6 \qquad \sqrt{64}$$

$$32.75 \qquad -4\frac{1}{2} \qquad 3^3 \qquad 10^2 \qquad -60\frac{2}{5} \qquad 0.01$$

$$\frac{97}{20} \qquad \sqrt{169} \qquad 10\%$$

21. Make a number line that shows the numbers from 500 to 1,500. Label all the powers of 2 that fit between 500 and 1,500.

Writing

22. Answer the letter to Dr. Math.

> Dear Dr. Math,
>
> On my last math test, I figured out that $4^2 \times 4^2$ is 64. I was really proud of myself till the next day when I got the test back and the teacher said it was 256. I don't get it! What did I do wrong?
>
> Sincerely,
> Confused About Squares

STUDENT GALLERY

The Seeing and Thinking Mathematically project is based at Education Development Center, Inc. (EDC), Newton, MA, and was supported, in part, by the National Science Foundation Grant No. 9054677. Opinions expressed are those of the authors and not necessarily those of the National Science Foundation.

CREDITS: Photography: Don Johnson • Beverley Harper (cover). Illustrations: Rod Vass: pp. 2, 6, 14, 17, 19, 27, 35 • Manfred Geier: pp. 7, 9, 15, 18, 22, 31, 39.

Creative Publications and MathScape are trademarks or registered trademarks of Creative Publications.

© 1998 Creative Publications
1300 Villa Street, Mountain View, California 94041

Printed in the United States of America.

0-7622-0207-6

1 2 3 4 5 6 7 8 9 10 . 02 01 00 99 98 97